Hungarian Numbers

Hungarian Number Book with English Translations

- ➢ *This is a beautiful 24-page Number book for children of ages 4+ to learn HUNGARIAN Numbers*

- ➢ *8.5 X11 Inch Color Hungarian Number Book*

- ➢ *Perfect book for introducing kids to the HUNGARIAN Language/HUNGARIAN Numbers*

- ➢ *Other books in HUNGARIAN Language series include:*

  - ➢ HUNGARIAN ALPHABETS PICTURES & WORDS BOOK: HUNGARIAN Alphabet Color Picture book with Words and English Translations

  - ➢ HUNGARIAN ALPHABET COLORING BOOK

  - ➢ HUNGARIAN Alphabet COLOR Poster/chart (Physical and Digital)

Follow us on Facebook/Instagram/Pinterest/Etsy

Leave us your honest feedback and get your free download of Hungarian alphabet posture. Email us at: Publishing@vaparisystems.com

Hungarian Alphabet

A Alma — Apple	**Á** Ágy — Bed	**B** Banán — Banana	**C** Cica — Cat	**CS** Csuzli — Sling-shot
D Dió — Walnut	**DZ** Dzsóker — Joker	**DZS** Dzsem — Jam	**E** Egy — One	**É** Négy — Four
F Fagylat — Icecream	**G** Gomb — Sphere	**GY** Gyertya — Candle	**H** Hangya — Ant	**I** Idő — Time
Í Ír — Write	**J** Juh — Sheep	**K** Kutya — Dog	**L** Ló — Horse	**LY** Lyuk — Hole
M Macska — Cat	**N** Nap — Sun	**NY** Nyul — Rabbit	**O** Oroszlán — Lion	**Ó** Ódon — Ancient
Ö Göndör — Curly	**Ő** Kő — Stone	**P** Paradicsom — Tomato	**Q** Aquafóbia — Aquaphobia	**R** rajz — Drawing
S Sarok — Heel	**SZ** Szem — Eye	**T** Táska — Bag	**TY** Tyúk — Hen	**U** Uborka — Cucumber
Ú Újság — Newspaper	**Ü** Üveg — Glass	**Ű** Tű — Needle	**V** Vízforraló — Kettle	**W** Wc — Toilet
X Xilofon — Xylophone	**Y** Yamgyökér — Yam	**Z** Zongora — Piano	**ZS** Zsiráf — Giraffe	

Hungarian Alphabets

MAGYAR BÉCÉ

0

Nulla   Zero

1

Egy   One

2

Két   Two

3

Három   Three

4

Négy   Four

5

Öt   Five

6

Hat   Six

7

Hét   Seven

8

Nyolc   Eight

9

Kilenc   Nine

10

Tíz   Ten

11

Tizenegy   Eleven

12

Tizenkét

Twelve

13

Tizenhárom

Thirteen

14

Tizennégy   Fourteen

15

Tizenöt   Fifteen

16

Tizenhat   Sixteen

17

Tizenhét   Seventeen

18

Tizennyolc

Eighteen

19

Tizenkilenc

Nineteen

20

Húsz   Twenty

21

Huszonegy   Twenty One

22

Húszonkettő   Twenty Two

23

Huszonhárom   Twenty Three

24

Huszonnégy   Twenty Four

25

Huszonöt   Twenty Five

26

Huszonhat   Twenty Six

27

Huszonhét   Twenty Seven

28

Huszonnyolc   Twenty Eight

29

Huszonkilenc   Twenty Nine

30

Harminc   Thirty

40

Negyven   Fourty

50

Ötven   Fifty

60

Hatvan   Sixty

70

Hetven　　　Seventy

80

Nyolcvan　　　Eighty

90

Kilencven   Ninty

100

Száz   Hundred

1,000

Ezer   Thousand

100,000

Százezer   Hundred Thousand

Million

Millió   Million

Hungarian Alphabet
Poster

Hungarian Alphabet
Picture Book

Hungarian English
First 100 words
Picture Book

Hungarian Alphabet

A Alma — Apple	**Á** Ágy — Bed	**B** Banán — Banana	**C** Cica — Cat	**CS** Csuzli — Sling-shot
D Dió — Walnut	**DZ** Dzsóker — Joker	**DZS** Dzsem — Jam	**E** Egy — One	**É** Négy — Four
F Fagylat — Icecream	**G** Gomb — Sphere	**GY** Gyertya — Candle	**H** Hangya — Ant	**I** Idő — Time
Í Ír — Write	**J** Juh — Sheep	**K** Kutya — Dog	**L** Ló — Horse	**LY** Lyuk — Hole
M Macska — Cat	**N** Nap — Sun	**NY** Nyul — Rabbit	**O** Oroszlán — Lion	**Ó** Ódon — Ancient
Ö Göndör — Curly	**Ő** Kő — Stone	**P** Paradicsom — Tomato	**Q** Aquafóbia — Aquaphobia	**R** rajz — Drawing
S Sarok — Heel	**SZ** Szem — Eye	**T** Táska — Bag	**TY** Tyúk — Hen	**U** Uborka — Cucumber
Ú Újság — Newspaper	**Ü** Üveg — Glass	**Ű** Tű — Needle	**V** Vízforraló — Kettle	**W** Wc — Toilet
X Xilofon — Xylophone	**Y** Yamgyökér — Yam	**Z** Zongora — Piano	**ZS** Zsiráf — Giraffe	

Hungarian Alphabets

MAGYAR BÉCÉ

Printed in Great Britain
by Amazon

23702026R10016